Sharon Coan

Publishing Credits

Rachelle Cracchiolo, M.S.Ed., *Publisher*
Conni Medina, M.A.Ed., *Managing Editor*
Jamey Acosta, *Content Director*
Dona Herweck Rice, *Series Developer*
Robin Erickson, *Multimedia Designer*

Image Credits: Cover, p.1 ©Kuttig - People/Alamy; pp.8, 12 ©iStock.com/Sharon Meredith; p.10 ©iStock.com/Ashok Rodrigues; pp.11-12 ©iStock.com/hockeymom4; all other images from Shutterstock.

Library of Congress Cataloging-in-Publication Data

Coan, Sharon, author.
Pushes and pulls / Sharon Coan.
pages cm
Summary: "Push or pull? This book shows you how pushing and pulling helps work get done."--Provided by publisher.
Audience: K to grade 3
ISBN 978-1-4938-2052-8 (pbk.)
1. Force and energy--Juvenile literature. I. Title.
QC73.4.C5185 2016
531.6--dc23

2015011883

Teacher Created Materials
5301 Oceanus Drive
Huntington Beach, CA 92649-1030
http://www.tcmpub.com

ISBN 978-1-4938-2052-8

Words to Know

pull

push